LBJ
A Foreign Observer's Viewpoint

LBJ

A Foreign Observer's Viewpoint

by

Michael Davie

DUELL, SLOAN AND PEARCE
New York

First edition

DUELL, SLOAN & PEARCE
AFFILIATE OF
MEREDITH PRESS

Library of Congress Catalog Card Number: 66-17040

MANUFACTURED IN THE UNITED STATES OF AMERICA
FOR MEREDITH PRESS

VAN REES PRESS • NEW YORK

LBJ
A Foreign Observer's Viewpoint

THE President comes into a room slowly and warily, as if he means to smell out the allegiance of everyone in it. He is big, a hulking six feet three, and despite a definite paunch and the recurrent anxieties about his health, he looks like a man with exceptional physical stamina. There is a faint air of the barroom strategist. The face is unprepossessing. The ears are huge, with long hanging lobes; the brow is a mass of complicated furrows; the mouth is a straight line. He dresses like a man who has told the best tailor in town to fit him out like a pillar of the chamber of commerce. When he shakes your hand (his own hand is capacious, hard, and brown, with a long vein down the back), he gives you the politician's sincere look straight between the eyes. His manner is restrained. His voice usually is very quiet, with a pronounced Southern accent, saying "strawng" for "strong." Afterward, you chiefly remember the small eyes, steady and unrelenting under half-lowered lids.

3

Ol' Lyndon, from the dirt-poor hill country of central Texas, is now a man of power, and the atmosphere and trappings of power always surround him, unconcealed and flagrant. At intervals throughout the day, huge helicopters, on the President's business, whirr over the heads of the tourists onto the White House lawn. Hidden tape recorders revolve in his private office. The windows he looks through are inches thick. When he gets into a car, he is always part of a motorcade. When he goes to church in Johnson City, large tanned men with guns sit in the pews and watch the congregation—mainly old ladies—over their prayer books. Wherever he travels, busloads of journalists follow him. When his plane takes off, a planeload of reporters and photographers waits to see if it will crash. When he is at his ranch in Texas, nearby roads are closed. At the ranch itself a communications mast smothered with aerials reaches up into the sky, helicopters stand round the farmyard as well as on the adjacent airstrip, and men in open-neck shirts carrying walkie-talkies patrol the garden.

For his convenience, when he swims at the ranch, a telephone floats in the pool. When he leaves

Texas to return to Washington, his big jet leaves from Bergstrom Air Force Base, where rows of silver, droop-winged B-52's—each of them, it is said, able to carry more firepower than was used during the whole of the Second World War—stand waiting in the sun for his orders. All this is visible; but it is only a fragment by comparison with what is invisible. Under his hand, besides, he has the silent Polaris submarines, the many-titled missiles, the hundreds of thousands of tight-lipped American troops. This is the master of the button. This is the master of our life and death.

He is one of the most extraordinary human beings ever to become President of the United States. He is more interesting, because infinitely more complex, than Kennedy. To meet him is to be awed and excited. He is purely and aggressively American, the first uninhibited product of the American frontier to take over since Andrew Jackson came out of Tennessee with his long white hair and sparky talk to beat the British at the Battle of New Orleans and become the first People's President.

Johnson had not long been in office before Washington became obsessed by him. All Presidents, naturally, preoccupy the capital, but with Johnson it was more than a preoccupation.

Washingtonians assumed, to begin with, that they knew all about him, since he had been around town for twenty-four years as Congressman and Senator and three years as Vice-President; but they gradually became aware that he was an infinitely more mysterious, complex, and formidable character than they had realized. At the same time, the capital observed Johnson's gradually establishing himself as one of the most powerful Presidents in American history. Kennedy, toward the end of his life, was running into a legislative impasse with Congress. A distinguished professor, James MacGregor Burns, who had been Kennedy's biographer, published a book in 1963 alarmingly called *The Deadlock of Democracy*, which argued that the antique governmental machine had at last jammed with age and must be radically overhauled to prevent an overmighty Congress from frustrating Presidential policies. The professor's opinion was widely shared at that time in Washington. But Johnson had scarcely settled in office before bills were coming out of Congress like candy bars from a slot machine, and other professors now began to wonder whether it was healthy for a President, with Congress dominated by Democrats and the Republican Party in disarray, to be subject to so few checks on his absolute dominion. By the middle of 1965, the President's position was indeed imperial. He could have dismissed the most famous of his subordinates and scarcely a Congressman would have squeaked. And as his power developed, so Washington's obsession with him developed, too. "Under Kennedy, it used to be ideas," remarked a columnist's wife, explaining why her dinner-party guests had spent the whole evening gossiping about Johnson. "Now it's all personality."

Having wandered round the city and noted that the capital's interest in the President's character and behavior seemed exceptionally intense, a visitor to the White House not long ago was at first struck by the thought that the atmosphere inside the building was more normal than it was outside. Secretaries gossiped on the telephone—"She was a real lovely bride...."—while a fellow in an open-neck shirt walked about with two dogs at his heels, Him, the most famous beagle in the world, and a white collie named Blanco, after Blanco County in Texas. The secretaries cooed over Blanco and cuddled him, becoming covered with long white hairs.

Before long, however, the peculiarities of the man in the center began to ripple outward.

First, there was the uncouthness, along with the dazzling ability, revealed in the minor personal traits. He picked his nose. He was liable, when slumped down in a chair, to reach casually and unashamedly into his groin to ease his pants. His phrasing was of a kind not usually associated with the Presidency of the United States. To a reporter who began an interview with a trivial question, he said, "Why do you come and ask me, the leader of the Western world, a chicken-shit question like that?" When the handsome and dignified Italian Secretary of NATO, Signor Manlio Brosio, came on a visit to Strategic Air Command in Nebraska, the President invited the accompanying reporters in the plane to come and talk with Mr. Brosio. As they settled down to question the distinguished guest, the President stood up. "I'm going to have a piss," he explained.

Then there are the stories of how he treats his subordinates. "Physically, he is extremely wound up," a member of the White House staff explained. "He gets rid of his head of steam by going for his subordinates. He builds up this tremendous energy inside himself, and something has to go." Whoever is nearest, male or female, gets the blast. "He doesn't appreciate the effect on other people's feelings. He'll bawl the ass off anyone—I mean, anyone—and he can use quite violent language." Some staff members comfort themselves with the notion that a Presidential lashing proves he trusts them. One distinguished subordinate greeted a man whom he knew to have been bawled out by the President with the words, intended as salve for the wound, "Welcome to the club." At least one White House man makes it a rule to keep out of the President's peripheral vision. It is typical of Johnson that no one is quite sure whether these rages, which may be quite prolonged, like a prowling thunderstorm, are uncontrolled or not. Some people claim to have seen him become enraged, then break off to have a calm telephone call, and then resume the bawling-out. They compare him with a man who is impelled to write furious letters for the wastebasket. Others recall that Winston Churchill's bursts of temper,

9

during World War II, were no less wounding or sudden than Johnson's and were similarly directed, sometimes, at very distinguished targets. Like Churchill, too, Johnson declines to recognize normal office hours, even if things are quiet, and expects his staff to be instantly available in the flesh when he wants them. One man, on a slack day, ventured to keep a lunch appointment at a hotel within ten minutes' walk of the White House. He had barely started his meal when he was telephoned by the President, to whom he explained that for once he was lunching out in a hotel. "What's the matter with the White House canteen?" asked the President. Some of his staff eat at their desks, off trays, at the ready.

The pride of the President is as open as a wound. One of his personal henchmen, Jack J. Valenti, delivered a speech before the Advertising Federation of America in June, 1965, referring to the President as "a cultivated man," giving examples of his "extraordinarily sophisticated diplomacy," and saying that "the President, thank the good Lord, has extra glands." Washington writhed in embarrassment, but the President thought the tone was about right. On another occasion, in Kansas City, Johnson telephoned former President Truman, asking him to breakfast the next day at seven. "Why so late, Lyndon?" asked Truman. Next morning Johnson rose at dawn to take a quick walk round the town, evidently so that he could be on the steps of his hotel when Truman arrived and upstage him by boasting that he'd been up and exercising for hours. Truman at the time was eighty-one.

Connected with Johnson's pride is his unconcealed desire to be loved. He wants everyone to vote for him all the time, and he is abnormally sensitive to criticism. When he is under fire from the press, his immediate instinct is to reach for his polls: the papers may sneer, but 63.5 per cent of the people love him. "He hates to be alone," said one staff member, "he really hates it"; and he battles continually against the inherent loneliness of his position. Under the Kennedys, the family rooms in The Mansion—the central block of the White House that figures on the postcards—were kept strictly private: even Mrs. Johnson, then the Vice-President's wife, rarely visited this part of the building. Under Johnson, anyone can get in; he and Mrs.

Johnson have regularly taken groups through on conducted tours. He has given a party for all congressmen and their wives, and, not content with that, for all congressmen's secretaries. He treats the press lobby in the White House almost as if it were an extension of his own office. He wanders around. Not long ago he wandered right out of the White House garden and into the Department of Commerce, where he delivered an impromptu talk to such people as happened to be present on the importance of the Department. One of his hearers subsequently wrote to the White House in gratitude, remarking that it was the first time he had set eyes on a President, in the line of work, for twenty years.

Johnson likes to get up close to people and recharge his batteries with their delight in meeting him. It seemed to give him special pleasure, once, when he went looking for tourists and astonished a group of high school girls from his home state, who sang for him "The Eyes of Texas Are Upon You." However, as a man who has known him ever since he arrived in Washington has pointed out, his search for affection does not get a clear run for its money. "His desire to be loved," said this man, "conflicts with his desire to project an image of power."

In pursuit of this image, according to one of his staff, Johnson "plays the Presidential thing to the hilt. If he wants to go to Texas, he goes the minute he wants to go; and he expects Air Force One to be there ready, with the engines running." No President has ever taken over the office with more prior knowledge of its powers than Johnson; and no President either, it is safe to add, has ever thrown himself onto the levers with more relish. Whether or not he has "extra glands," as Mr. Valenti believes, he certainly has "vast energies," as Theodore C. Sorensen has testified since he left the President's service. Johnson himself is said to consider that the margin he has over other men is his capacity to work harder than they do; the extraordinary energy with which he sets about his duties suggests a determination to keep the margin as wide as possible.

The President normally wakes at seven thirty and works in bed for about two hours before he goes, around ten, to his calm, beautiful, and womb-like oval office in the West Wing for the day's action. He takes a late lunch break, sometimes swimming in the pool, and regularly sleeps (getting into pajamas) in the afternoon. Around five, he begins his "second day," working on in his office until ten or eleven at night, if he has no evening appointments, and occasionally later. When he turns in, he finds waiting for him on his bed two or three hours' worth of "night reading"—stacks of bulky brown envelopes containing what the White House categorizes as "reports from State and Defense, the latest intelligence reports, cables from ambassadors, memoranda from various Cabinet officers and White House staff members, budget data, project reports from task forces working on various problems, magazine articles, newspaper clippings and personnel recommendations, as well as selected samples of the day's mail," much of it requiring his scribbled comments. During one week, according to Mr. Valenti's sums, the President's night reading (which is also his early-morning reading) normally adds up to "the equivalent of a 100,000 word novel" —and this is quite apart from what he consumes in his office.

"The President is a very restless man," says one of his staff. "The President is a wary man," adds another. Both these characteristics affect his method of work. He is a keen telephone user, and at any hour of the day or night telephones are liable to ring in Washington and a relaxed voice may say, "This is Lyndon. Ah have a problem." A record is kept of the President's calls, and on the occasions when he has felt it helpful to make this record public, as he did after the Dominican crisis, when he had been criticized for acting without proper consultation, the figures he has produced have been startlingly high.

"One of the keys to Lyndon Johnson is that he is a perfectionist—a perfectionist in the most imperfect art in the world: politics," remarks an old associate. "He has a passion for detail and a mastery of detail. Decision-making, he gets all the information, wants to know every point of view, leaves the decision as long as possible, and then decides—strong, firm and to the jugular." Some people have deduced from Johnson's actions, as in the Dominican Republic, for instance, that he is an impulsive man, but this old associate denies it. "I doubt if Lyndon ever did anything impulsive in his life," he says. A White House man in regular contact with the President agrees: "He is always rest-lessly searching for solutions to problems, and he gets things on his mind; but he doesn't act impul-sively, though it might look like that from outside. He ruminates." Confronted by a request for a rapid decision or the release of information, the Presi-dent's instinct, apparently, is to ask who it is that's pressing for a decision, what's his reason, and, if unconvinced by the answer, to hold the matter for a while to await Presidential brooding. He insists on making every decision he can himself. His staff have learned that no detail is too trivial to check with him. On occasion, when news of minor de-partmental appointments has leaked out before he could father the announcement himself, he has can-celed the appointments. Some of his staff feel that his wariness causes him needless anxiety. "Some of his worries are of his own making," one man re-marked. "He sees troubles where none exist. He's liable to wake up in the morning and think every-thing's got loose during the night." Another ex-plained: "He sees life as a jungle. No matter how long a rein you think you're on, he's always got the reins in his own hands."

Because Johnson's method of work tends to involve other people, whom he summons as he wants them, his office can seem peculiarly disorderly. He will conduct several conversations at the same time, taking in (one is assured) the meaningful parts of each. If he gets bored, he may pick up the telephone and call someone else on a different topic, subsequently taking up an earlier discussion at the point where he interrupted it. Or he may suddenly remember that there is something on television he must see and without apology switch on his triple-screen set, he and his visitors sitting silently through a commercial until the program comes on. He shows an evident impatience with the polite conversational bows with which nervous strangers are liable to open their meetings with him. Nor does he encourage abstract talk for its own sake: "He doesn't like to get into discussions before he can, as he puts it, 'move in the stack,' " explains an adviser. In this, he differs strikingly from his predecessor. Kennedy, in the phrase of one of his advisers, "used to suck up foreigners like a vacuum cleaner," but Johnson, on the contrary, tries to dodge them, unless there is some specific deal to be made. His advisers have particularly discouraged stray calls from foreign statesmen who want to lecture the President on American foreign policy, or whose main purpose is to use their visit to the President, plus the pictures of themselves in smiling accord on the White House steps, to make a political impression back home. British Prime Ministers, especially, have played this game for years.

When Johnson does get involved, however, he becomes deeply immersed, cross-questioning experts, surprising them with his memory and powers of concentration and simplifying problems until he is sure he grasps them. In these sessions, his advisers note, the President's political antennae are invariably fully extended. "He's thinking of the political implications three months ahead."

Johnson rarely plays. Kennedy had personal friends outside politics with whom he insisted on keeping up. It is doubtful whether Johnson has any idea what "outside politics" means. "When he goes boating on that lake down in Texas, the people he has along are people he has a reason for wanting to talk to."

Not everyone agrees that these methods of work

18

are perfect. In the White House there are those—Johnsonist loyalists though they are—who consider that the President is willful and who feel that advice, sometimes, doesn't get through to him. If he is convinced that a particular course of action is the right one, he is inclined to regard attempts to divert him from that course, however well intentioned, as sabotage.

These defects seem minor, however, by comparison with the massive testimony available on the sheer talent of the overall Presidential performance. He is no abstract thinker, and no idealist; but he may well be, as a former member of his Congressional staff believes, "the ablest President of this century." One of his closest associates puts it thus, "You can divide Presidents into two classes, the architects and the engineers. Kennedy was an architect; he saw the overall design and drew up the plans. Johnson is an engineer, possibly the greatest engineer in the history of the United States." A third admirer employed a more lyrical imagery: "Toscanini was a great conductor, right? He knew what the second violin could do, what the brass could do, what the whole orchestra could do. That's like

Lyndon. He knows what each person and each group can do and what it can't do. He's a political artist of genius."

Analyzing the political skills the President possesses, one man said, "His great secret is that he knows men's motives. He knows exactly how far you will go to get what you want. He knows what you want, and he knows what I want, and he can put you and me together and make us realize that we can get things together that we can't get if we operate separately. He knows, as they say, where the bones are buried. He believes men are moved by influence, not argument. If he wants a Congressman to do something, he'll know enough about him to know that the person with the greatest influence on him is, say, a Minister; and then he'll get someone to persuade the Minister to persuade the Congressman." His powers of persuasion are indeed unrivaled. "Every time I see Lyndon," a journalist once complained, "he talks me out of six columns."

Johnson's political art was perfected during eight years as Majority Leader in the Congress—one of the most skillful, if not *the* most skillful, ever known there. Even as President, when his old stage on Capitol Hill has expanded to include the entire world, he still likes nothing better than to take up his old baton and conduct a piece of legislative hocus-pocus in person. Some months ago his legislative team, realizing that much of the legislation that had been passing Congress so smoothly was old New Deal legislation which had been around for years, felt it was time for a new, specifically Johnsonian item to be put through as well, to prove that it could be done. They came up with a bill to subsidize the rents of low-income families. The President approved, and they went to work to gather the votes. When they started, they knew that their total number of solid backers scarcely exceeded double figures, but step by step they gradually collected support until at last they were within fourteen of the two hundred or so votes needed. And there, threaten and argue as they might, they stuck: the thing was impossible. Up stepped the old maestro to the podium. For four solid hours one morning, from seven until eleven, he was on the telephone in his bedroom; when he emerged, he had the votes. That night, reviewing his achievement with his staff, he was exultant. "They talk about ca-jolery and per-suasion," he exclaimed in a high state of exhilaration, "but this mawning it was sheer horsepower." Giving this account later, one of his staff remarked: "If I'm calculating votes, I'm either too optimistic or too pessimistic. But the President is unillusioned. He can count."

In pursuing what he wants, from legislators or anyone else, the President rarely attacks head on any adversaries who may be across his path. He likes to keep the tone of politics pitched low, and prides himself on his self-restraint toward opponents and detractors. During the 1964 Presidential election campaign he refrained, in spite of extreme provocation, from hitting Senator Goldwater with the rabbit punch that might have snapped the Senator's political career in two, preferring instead to let him finish himself off. Nor has the President once let slip, publicly, even a *sotto voce* riposte to the haughty rebukes and insults tossed across the Atlantic by President de Gaulle. He once complained privately of the Chinese, who abuse the United States regularly and without inhibition, that "they spit in your eye," but he has not allowed either himself or his lieutenants to answer them in comparable terms. For a man with a public reputation for crudity—and who is the head of the most powerful nation in the world—the tone of his utterances on foreign affairs has been notably dulcet.

His preferred methods of dealing with his critics have been nowhere better shown than over his most criticized policy, the conduct of the war in Vietnam. Confronted by one critic, he would talk about his other critics, often with an air of self-pity for all the burdens he as President was carrying, so that the critic found himself unwittingly drawn to Johnson's side. Or he employed the rebuff direct. To an Ambassador who brought up Vietnam, he said, "How many troops have yo' all got in Vietnam?" Or he appealed for help: "Ah'm tryin' everything I can." He asked senators to send him private memos, instead of making speeches. When the *New York Times* printed critical editorials, he rang up the paper and asked them what they proposed instead. "On Vietnam," said one of his visitors, "he makes you feel he's going through storms for the sake of righteousness. He makes you want to burst into generous tears." There is, besides, the celebrated tale of how he met Senator Frank Church of Idaho, a critic, at a gathering and put an arm round his shoulder.

"Frank," he said, "that speech yo' made wasn't one bit helpful."

"I'm sorry, Mr. President, the headlines exaggerated what I said."

"The headlines were all Ah read, Frank, and they're all the people read."

"But I didn't go any further than Walter Lippmann."

"Well, Frank," he said, sorrowfully, "the next time you need money to build a dam in your state, you better go to Mr. Lippmann."

This story has been polished and repolished by Washington legend, but it deserves to become a classic, for it embalms in its few exchanges some typically Johnsonian attitudes—the friendliness, the self-pity, the identification of himself with the people, and the sudden alarming glint of power.

Another facet of the many-sided Presidential performance is the care he takes in fitting the right people into the right jobs. Being himself a professional, Johnson has a strong bias toward other professionals in government. He has established an elaborate system for screening all new appointments —for expertise, not loyalty—and some think he is more painstaking at finding the right men than was Kennedy. After so many years in Washington, the President is perfectly familiar with all the "networks" except in the field of foreign affairs, where he has sometimes been compelled, in looking for ambassadors and other external operatives, to rely on the opinions of others. In the process of tooling up his own personal governmental machine he has shown himself much less ready than his predecessors to employ talented amateurs with no direct experience in government. It is inconceivable, for instance, that he could ever make an appointment such as President Eisenhower made when he sent as Ambassador to Ceylon the incurious Maxwell Henry Gluck, a contributor to Republican Party funds who turned out not to know the name of the Ceylonese Prime Minister. Johnson was genuinely taken aback not long ago when he discovered by chance that one middle-aged member of his entourage—a man of great skill at the job—had been in government less than two years. He could scarcely credit that someone with so brief an experience of Washington on the inside could be efficient.

Both the President's methods and his performance are, to say the least, out of the ordinary, marking him off as an exceptional man, even an oddity; but the most extraordinary feature of his character is that he feels an outsider in Washington. "He doesn't feel, even now, that he belongs here," explained one of the aides who knows him best. "From the beginning of his career he was an outsider looking in—a country boy without education and without money. He's always felt that people from his part of the country have had a raw deal, and he always felt he was being looked down on. He still feels it. He's got to be President and yet he feels he hasn't made it. This is the cause of most of his frustrations and erraticisms."

The President's integration into his own capital has not been helped by the hierarchical and self-regarding nature of Washington. The city has a Southern flavor and a high proportion of Negro citizens; but the section that counts politically is overwhelmingly dominated by Northern, and even European, attitudes and manners. Johnson is a

Southerner, and, as the late A. J. Liebling once re-marked, Southern politicians travel badly, like sweet corn. By the time they reach the cities to the north they have become overripe, offending delicate Northern palates. This is what has happened to Johnson. In Washington, with its squads of diplo-mats, civil servants, and college-educated graduates, he shocks them. It is true, as a friend of Johnson has pointed out, that there are many more people in the United States like Lyndon than there are like Dean Acheson, and that the Acheson-type territory is only a sliver of the whole country; but Wash-ington is part of the sliver. There they find his aura crude. They disapprove when he scratches, or abuses people, or employs bad language. They are bored by his taste for telling long "Ah-recall-mah-cousin-Aliza-once" type of stories; they preferred the Kennedy wit to the Johnson humor. When the First Lady serves raspberry icebox pie or Texas bean soup, they make clever jokes about her. For a long time Washington could scarcely believe that the fellow in charge was really Ol' Lyndon. He was the most powerful man in the world, but to Wash-ington he still seemed very provincial.

The President knows what Washington feels about him. And the knowledge makes him bitter. He does his best. He tries to modify his Southern accent. He reduces the expansiveness of his gestures. But it's no use, and he is aware of that, too. "You're no one in this town," he burst out on one occasion, "unless you dine once a week with the Alphands." Hervé Alphand was at that time the French ambassador, and again the President was giving himself away as an outsider. The Alphands had already been supplanted as the leaders of Washington society.

The President attributes the capital's rejection of himself to regional prejudice. He thinks they don't approve of him because he comes from Texas. In return he feels about Washington, and the East Coast three-button-suit crowd generally, that they are a bunch of snobs who look down their noses at you while they are stealing your wallet. The people the President likes are the people. In the White House, he and his Texan entourage feel cut off from the people by three groups: by the press, which they think is inflated by a misguided sense of its own importance; by the Congress, which represents the people but is not the people; and by the lobbyists, who look after the interests of groups that are well looked after already.

This outsider quality in Johnson has contributed to his imperfect relations with the Kennedy family and their adherents, and with the Washington press corps. He failed, from the beginning of his Presidency, to persuade the Kennedyites to transfer to him the intense political loyalty they had had for the late President. It soon became plain that there was, as one ringside observer put it, "an emotional block" between Johnson and Robert Kennedy. Mrs. Kennedy, too, despite regular, solicitous telephone calls from the White House, has declined to respond to Johnson's advances; instead, a widowed queen in exile, she waits on Fifth Avenue for the restoration of the dynasty to the throne. Gradually, as Johnson's first year of elected office drew on, the Kennedys began to emerge as the opposition within the Democratic Party. The Kennedyites, particularly the intellectuals, similarly drifted away outside the Johnson orbit; "the Kennedy years were magic, and the magic lasted all the time he was President," explained the wife of one of them; "but this man—he's creepy." This was a personal, feminine reaction from someone who used to be inside the Kennedy circle, but there were deeper reasons for this disaffection. Kennedy, though not an intellectual himself, publicly and privately recognized intellectual caliber, attracted intellectuals to Washington, and gave them a heady whiff of power. Their historic status in the United States had always been ambiguous; in the previous decade they had experienced the hostility of unchecked McCarthyism, and they had felt totally remote from what many of them regarded as the mindlessness of the Eisenhower Administration. Under Kennedy, the whole tribe felt that at last the claims of intellect were being recognized and that they had an opportunity to contribute directly to the conduct of their nation's affairs. Pablo Casals played and Nobel prize winners were honored at the White House; Harvard professors were employed as personal advisers and emissaries of the President. What a revolution from the days when Eisenhower, in 1954, mockingly defined an intellectual as "a man who takes more words than are necessary to tell more than he knows"!

Under Johnson, however, the intellectuals soon began to feel that if the new Administration was not as philistine and anti-intellectual as Eisenhower's, it was at any rate much less sympathetic than Kennedy's. No one, except Valenti, has ever claimed that Lyndon Johnson is a cultivated man; the White House, instead of trying to stimulate the pursuit of excellence, seemed to have reverted to corn, and the general style of Johnsonian leadership seemed sweaty and crude. The intellectuals under Kennedy had been enthralled by the spectacle of the exercise of power; under Johnson, they snapped back into their more traditional posture of suspicion and disenchantment. Like the Brahmins when Andrew Jackson, "the unlettered man of the West, the nursling of the wilds," came clomping into Washington as the people's candidate to oust John Quincy Adams and "government by gentlemen," so the Kennedyites felt unable to come to terms with Johnson. When Harvard awarded President Jackson an honorary degree in 1833, Henry Adams wrote that he *"would not* be present to see my darling Harvard disgrace herself by conferring a Doctor's degree upon a barbarian and savage who

31

can scarcely spell his own name." Some Kennedyites had not dissimilar feelings about Johnson, and
these, originally perhaps cultural, were turned political by the persistence of the war in Vietnam, so
that by the summer of 1965 public criticism of the
President's policies seemed for a time to be coming
almost entirely from university faculty members
who had been pro-Kennedy.

When Johnson attempted to take a leaf out of
Kennedy's book and close the gap between himself
and the intellectuals by holding a cultural rally in
the White House garden, he only made things
worse. Robert Lowell, the poet, refused to go, and
Dwight Macdonald in the *New York Review of
Books* wrote a long, mocking account of the occasion. Shortly afterward playwright Arthur Miller,
whom both the President and Mrs. Johnson were
said to admire, delivered an eloquent public attack
on the Administration's Vietnamese policy. This
had to be answered by the State Department. But
in practice the White House was far more hos-
pitable to intellectuals than the hundred-per-cent
Kennedyites were ready to concede. Two of Kennedy's best-known Harvard imports, Professors

J. K. Galbraith and Arthur Schlesinger, Jr., had, it is true, soon withdrawn, but two others, W. W. Rostow and McGeorge Bundy, stayed on. Both of them, it might be added, became more influential under Johnson than they had been under Kennedy —Rostow at the State Department and Bundy, spectacles and intelligence flashing, as the President's right-hand man on foreign affairs; until Bundy left office early in 1966, each of these men was more influential than either Schlesinger, who worked in the East Wing while Kennedy worked in the West Wing, or Galbraith, who worked principally in India, had ever been during Kennedy's heyday. Besides, even the Texans brought in by Johnson were by no means the slow-footed louts that some of the Kennedyites liked to make them out to be, and one or two of them, tucked away unsung in the back offices of the White House, could have come out and gone ten rounds with the nimblest of the East Coast champions. When the Kennedyites compared Johnson unfavorably with their hero, the Johnsonites were inclined to reply, as we have seen, that Kennedy was an architect, whereas their man was an engineer, or that Kennedy was running into a cul-de-sac with Congress, whereas their man had pushed through a legislative revolution. Here was another echo of the clash between Adams and Andrew Jackson: the Johnsonians in 1965 were using a variant of the defense used by the Jacksonian who remarked, when comparing the records of the two Presidents, "Jackson made law; Adams quoted it."

Besides the Kennedyites, Johnson has also had difficulties with the press. In seeking for favorable contacts with newspapermen, the President and his advisers have tried every method they could think of: formal press conferences with the reporters on gilt chairs and TV cameras live; sudden invitations to "my friends out there" (in the press lobby) to enter the Presidential office, with him "buying coffee"; long walks round the garden; barbecues at the ranch; small lunches; invitations to the White House family rooms (where a lady reporter once caught sight of him in his underpants); and intimate conversations in the small study off his main office. Yet Johnson's press relations have continued to grate.

He has thanked reporters, complained to them,

and refused altogether to see one of the most distinguished, Theodore H. White. When he tried to please reporters by taking some of them for a ride round the ranch in his car, all he achieved was a front-page story about his allegedly dangerous driving. The most notable outcome of a party he gave for journalists and their families on the White House lawn was a comic piece in the *New York Times*.

What is wrong? In the view of one professional in this field, the President's basic error is to confuse press relations with public relations. "He thinks that if you put funny hats on their heads and give them a barbecue, they'll treat you right. It was the same when he was a Senator; he'd sit up half the night drinking with some hostile reporter and then be surprised when the reporter stayed hostile." He does not realize that the technique that pleases congressmen and gets results—Presidential invitations, flattery, promises of future favors, and scrupulousness in thanking people for their help—doesn't necessarily work with reporters. A Congressman, however independent-minded, can scarcely help being gratified when the President of the United States

35

singles him out at some gathering to thank him for his invaluable help with a bill; he will be ready to give the President another hand in the future. On the contrary, a reporter who is told that the President liked a story is liable to think—if he is a good reporter—that there must have been something wrong with the story.

Johnson does not appear to realize that a reporter's main yearning is to know what's going on and to print it. One celebrated reporter who went to see the President about Vietnam told his friends afterward that the President had pulled out a list of all the countries he had visited as Vice-President, as evidence of his experience in foreign affairs, but his face had hardened into rock when the reporter started asking about the war. As a former Administration press secretary summed up: "Kennedy treated reporters as grown-ups and equals and knew that they and he were in a different kind of business; Johnson seems to think it's strange that he can't have the reporters in his pocket."

As with the Kennedyites, too, there exists a kind of cultural bar between Johnson and some members of the Washington press corps. Covering the glamorous Kennedy, who always made them feel important, was a dignified assignment for them. "We made him and we can break him," one exhilarated television commentator told his colleagues in a press bus following Kennedy through Florida in 1961.

Dogging the steps of an uncouth fellow like Johnson, on the other hand, who sometimes makes them feel as if they were private detectives on a seedy divorce case, and who compels them to take regular trips to rural Texas instead of somewhere civilized like Palm Beach, arouses in some of them a deep subterranean resentment. "You know what I don't like about coming back to Austin? Coming back to Austin," an unexhilarated reporter told his colleagues in a press bus following Johnson into Texas in 1965.

Journalists covering Lyndon daily find him as hard to understand as everyone else does. "There is no journalistic formula by which the subtlety and complexity of this man can be conveyed," remarked one of his staff. He meant that Truman got cast as the "give-'em-hell-Harry" President, Eisenhower as "the captive hero" (in the phrase of Marquis

Childs), Kennedy as "the glamorous activist." But Johnson is full of paradoxes. He is a Southerner, and yet he has never quite fitted into the Southerner category; he is a Texan, yet he has been booed and jostled in Dallas as a "Yankee"; he bullies his staff, yet he stands up for them fiercely when they are under attack; he is a pure politician, the most political of all Presidents, yet somewhere deep down inside him he evidently recognizes that politics are only a means to an end; he is suspicious of East Coast intellectuals, yet Bundy of Harvard was for more than two years one of his most trusted key men; he dominates the nation, yet he feels insecure. Asked in Washington one day how these contradictions might be resolved, one of Johnson's shrewdest old friends replied: "Go west. The further west you go, the nearer you get to Lyndon Johnson."

THE President himself travels west whenever he can. He goes back where he came from, to the poor and arid hill country of central Texas. In Washington, he doubts whether he's made the grade. In Texas, on the banks of the little Pedernales River, he knows he has. Everywhere he looks he sees proof: the signs reading "Home Town of Lyndon B. Johnson," the LBJ notice on the gate of his ranch, the LBJ brand on his cattle, the LBJ birthplace, the LBJ boyhood home, the LBJ school, the LBJ television stations, the other LBJ ranches, and the recently renamed Lyndon B. Johnson Lake. Anyone who is anyone in this district, including the Governor, dines with the Johnsons. There are no foreign ambassadors around.

Down here, clues to the President's strange and contradictory personality begin to emerge.

He is a product of Texas, but a Texas little known to the outside world. There are no oil wells in this part of the state, no open plains, no high-heeled boots decorated with silver, no long-legged blondes buying diamond toys at Neiman-Marcus. This country is bleak. The nearest large town is Austin, an agreeable place where there are still a few old Southern colonial mansions, and where Mexicans stand at street corners on hot nights; but even Austin, although it is the state capital and is dominated by the huge red granite capitol building, ranks only sixty-seventh in size among American cities.

To get to the Johnson country, you drive west along a big wide highway for sixty miles. Outside Austin, beyond the geologically famous Balcones fault, the road soon starts to rise into irregular low hills scattered with stunted, bent, and scrawny trees. The topsoil is thin and stony. There are few animals and fewer people. The horizon is vast and endless, and the sun comes burning down from an enormous sky. There are caves full of bats. There are vultures and vicious diamondback rattlesnakes. The region is subject to droughts and floods. It is one of the hardest parts of the United States. "It is unrelenting country," Lady Bird Johnson once remarked, "and Lyndon is unrelenting, too."

Almost within living memory, this was the American frontier. Not much more than a hundred years ago the Indians still considered themselves masters of this land. They were too sensible to live here, using it instead as a hunting ground for deer and turkey, until they were driven out by the white man after a series of long and bloody battles that lasted, spasmodically, for forty years. As late as 1869 Johnson's grandmother, Eliza Bunton Johnson, hid in a space under the floor of her log cabin, gagging her baby with a diaper, while Comanche Indians, who had just scalped a neighbor nearby, smashed her wedding presents and ransacked the house overhead.

Johnson's ancestors helped to make Texan history. The family first came into the state from Georgia, as part of the great southwestward thrust of men and women who pushed into Texas to seek their fortunes—often with little more than an ax and a rifle—after the granting of statehood in 1845. A decade later, when the railways started to open up the West by building spurs out to the edge of the High Plains, Johnson's grandfather, Sam Ealy Johnson, was one of those who drove his cattle up the long, legendary trail from Texas to the railhead at Kansas City, where a good herd of longhorns, fed on the juicy grasses of the plains, might sell for a profit as high as 700 per cent. It was Sam Johnson who gave his name to the little settlement of Johnson City and built the thick stone walls, as a defense against the Comanches, that are now a prize feature of the LBJ ranch.

Sam Johnson lived to see Lyndon born. The contrast between his life and that of his son, Sam, Jr., Johnson's father, neatly illustrates a fundamental change in local history. The older Sam in his youth had been a cowboy who roamed the open range and slept under the stars wherever his cattle happened to be. By the time his son grew to manhood the open range had disappeared, carved up and fenced off by the new wave of settlers who poured into Texas along with the expanding railways. The range gave way to farms, and Johnson's father was a farmer. He was also a politician and member of the Texas Legislature, so that by the time Lyndon was born, in 1908, the name of Johnson was celebrated in the district. Even so, Lyndon grew up in hardship. His father was a smart politician but less smart as a farmer, and he unwisely put the family holdings into cotton. Johnson's birthplace is not much bigger than a three-car garage.

He left high school at fifteen, worked his way to California, returned home broke, and took a job with a road-building gang. Then his mother persuaded him to go back to school at Southwest Texas State Teachers College, and there he seems to have become aware of his powers. He received a degree when he was twenty-two, and spent two years teaching public speaking and debating in a Houston high school. Then he got a job that took him for the first time to Washington, as secretary to Congressman Richard M. Kleberg, one of the famous family who owned the colossal King Ranch.

You can still capture a strong flavor of those early Johnson days by visiting what is reverently known in Johnson City as "The Boyhood Home," where the Johnsons moved when Lyndon was five. It is a small, decent, single-story house of white-painted wood, with a rough lawn of crabgrass, a water tank on stilts in the garden, and a porch from which Johnson made one of his first political speeches. In this house you feel above all the presence of "Miz" Johnson, the President's mother. She was Rebekah Baines and she came from an educated Baptist family. Her grandfather was president of a Baptist university; her father was in Texas politics and ran a newspaper. Her furniture is still in the house: modest Victorian chairs upholstered in crimson plush, a gate-legged sewing table, a photograph of "my precious children," a few prized pieces of china, a small cupboard of heavily elaborate cut glass, and—her most valued possession—a chandelier of amethyst and crystal with mauve pendants and a windmill painted on the rim. She died in 1958. From all accounts, she was a deeply religious woman of great sweetness and strength of character. The emotional backing that she gave her son, who was devoted to her, may be deduced from the letter she wrote to him in 1937 after he ran for Congress at her insistence, and got in.

My darling Boy,

Beyond "Congratulations, Congressman," what can I say to my dear son in this hour of triumphant success? In this as in all the many letters I have written you there is the same theme: I love you; I believe in you; I expect great things of you.

To me your election not alone gratifies my pride as a mother in a splendid and satisfying son and delights me with the realization of the joy you must feel in your success, but in a measure it compensates for the heartache and disappointment I experienced as a child when my dear father lost the race you have just won. My confidence in the good judgment of the people was sadly shattered then by their choice of another man. Today my faith is restored. How happy it would have made my precious, noble father to know that the first-born of his first-born would achieve the position he was denied! It makes me happy to have you carry on the ideals and principles cherished by that great and good man. I gave you his name. I commend to you his example. You have always justified my expectations, my hopes, my dreams. How dear to me you are you cannot know, my darling boy, my devoted son, my strength and comfort.

Take care of yourself, darling. Write to me. Always remember that I love you and am behind you in all that comes to you. Kiss my dear children in Washington for me.

My dearest love,

Mother.

Besides "The Boyhood Home," there is another building in Johnson City that offers a glimpse into the community in which Johnson grew up. This is a neat, white-painted structure, down a dusty side road, with a notice in the front saying: "First Christian Church. Welcome." Peering into the opaque depths of the Presidential soul not long ago, one of his associates remarked: "Few people would agree with me, but I think the President has deep religious feeling. Of course, he doesn't give that impression. In fact, he gives the opposite impression."

Religious or not, the young Lyndon, who was brought up by his pious mother to be a Baptist, was moved at the age of fifteen, at about the same time that he was abandoning school against his mother's wishes, to leave the Baptists and join the Christian Churches (Disciples of Christ)—a Protestant denomination, founded in Kentucky during the early nineteenth century, that laid special emphasis on uniting all churches. Johnson is not the only member of his family to have changed his spiritual allegiance: his daughter Luci, who was brought up as an Episcopalian, became a Catholic; and his wife, brought up as a Methodist, became an Episcopalian.

Nowadays the President "likes to church-hop," as an aide puts it, but when he is spending a weekend at the ranch he often attends a Sunday morning service at the First Christian Church. Even if he wished to worship there unnoticed, which is open to doubt, the President could not do so. When he arrives with his motorcade he is swallowed up outside the church by a crowd of locals, gaping tourists, reporters, police, and television cameras. Inside, however, Johnson for once is cut off from the trappings of the Presidency. ". . . And the Spirit and the bride say, Come," intones the minister. "And he that heareth, let him say, Come. And he that is athirst, let him come; and whosoever will, let him take the water of life freely." He pauses, and there is absolute silence in the church except for the low drumming of the air conditioning, a gift of the President. Then the spruce boy at the piano strikes up the rousing old-time tune of "Sowing in the Morning," and as the rumbling voice of the President joins the rest of the congregation—the men ill at ease in their unfashionable suits, the old ladies proud under their elaborate hats—the atmosphere in the church seems suddenly much closer to the vanished frontier than to present-day Washington.

When the minister takes the floor to deliver his sermon, the connection between the President and the church seems still more plain, for the art of preaching the word of God and the art of political oratory are, in the West, allied. The big man wedged into the pew and the bespectacled minister, a row of pens in his breast pocket, both employ comparable techniques: the same beseeching, the same use of rambling stories from rural experience to make a point, the same wide-arm gestures, the same intense personal appeal to "each and every one of you." One of the preacher's constant themes is the search for Christian unity; it is conceivable that this central tenet of the Disciples of Christ (a pamphlet in the church notes that "the business of the Disciples is unity, and it should never be forced to the periphery of our concern") is connected by subterranean wiring to the President's own constant advocacy of the need for "consensus."

However this may be, there is no doubt that the President, on these churchgoing occasions in Johnson City, feels himself to be an intimate part of the small local community. "Ah was *looking* for you," he says to an old man after the service, gripping him above the elbow, and asks a small boy, "Are you Linda's brother?" Then, waving and smiling, he gets behind the wheel of his station wagon and leads his motorcade back to the ranch, the helicopters, and the decisions.

The community of Johnson City—a scattering of houses, mostly single story, among the scrub—is not much changed, except in its prosperity, since Johnson, a thin and eager youth, left it to go to Washington in the early thirties. He took with him a burden of local grievances. He resented the way the natural hardships of rural lives were increased by lack of irrigation and high interest rates, and he looked then, as he looks now, to the machinery of the Federal Government as the instrument of social improvement.

In these attitudes he was following his father and his father's friends. All these men were Populists. His father was born in 1877, at a time when the dream of the golden West was at its most optimistic and euphoric. To some extent the dream was artificially manufactured. The railways were opening up the West, and their need to populate the empty back country, both in order to sell off their vast land grants from the government and to ensure their own future prosperity, was causing them to advertise the easy money and climatic delights available west of the Mississippi with a lack of scruple unrivaled even in the history of American real-estate salesmanship. For a while, the West boomed; but by the end of the 1880's the bubble had burst. Prices of wheat, corn, and beef cattle had begun a decline that was to continue to the end of the century, and the seeds were being sown for the Populist Revolt. From Texas to the Dakota Territory, farmers felt cheated; they were, they proclaimed, the victims of a conspiracy "to rob the farmers of the fruits of their toil." As more and more of them got deep into debt and sank from yeomen farmers to tenant farmers or sharecroppers, they began to identify the conspirators. First, they blamed the railways, which monopolized the only means whereby the farmers could get their products to market, and which charged extortionate freight charges and favored the big men against the small; second, they attacked the trusts, which combined to fix prices on everything the back country needed, from seeds to clothes; and third, they blamed the bankers, who, they believed, deliberately maintained a shortage of dollars in order to extract more and bigger profits out of the soaring interest rates.

In the old days, aggrieved farmers had simply struck camp and headed further west. But by the end of the nineteenth century there was nowhere else to go. The railways, with the connivance of both central and state governments, had taken over all the land which formerly had been free—the land that, in the eyes of the farmers, was the rightful heritage of the American people as a whole. Trapped, the farmers began to organize. If the railways were protected by law, as they were, then the law must be changed; and changing the law meant getting into politics—meant raising less corn and more hell.

The first political seed of the revolt was planted by a group of Texas farmers in Lampasas County, the next county but one to Johnson City. From this seed sprang the Grand State Alliance of Texas, which expanded to become the Southern Alliance, which in turn combined with the North West Alliance, and in 1892 joined with other groups to form the People's (or Populist) Party, which advocated cheap money ("free silver"), the nationalization of the railways, laws to end speculation in farm produce, the recovery of the railway land grants, and national aid for irrigation. Four years later William Jennings Bryan, endorsed by both Democrats and Populists, became a candidate for the Presidency, fighting the alarmed Republicans drawn up in defense of property rights and gold. Bryan was defeated, however, and with his defeat died the Populist hopes of becoming an effective third party. By 1898 only in Texas did the Populists make a showing at the polls that compared favorably with previous years.

But the Populist movement was not an isolated phenomenon; it was only one more example of the way the politics of the frontier have constantly shaped the history of the United States. The friends of Johnson's father were part of a tradition that went back to the American Revolution, which was itself in part a frontier rebellion against long-range control. Jeffersonian democracy had its roots in the notion, particularly palatable on the frontier, that the common man had the right to be his own master, and embodied a profound suspicion of the great landed proprietors and merchant capitalists; and Andrew Jackson, who brought to an end the rule of the East Coast, European-oriented grandees, was himself a typical child of the frontier. In all these movements of American history there were the same ingredients: a protest of the ordinary man against the dominance of the great and wealthy; an acceptance of inflationist theories of finance (the paper-money revolt of the farmers led by Daniel Shays, the banking laws of Jackson, the free-silver cry of the Populists); and a dislike of absentee rule. None of these movements had any strong desire to overturn the basis of society. Each of them represented an attempt by the outsiders to redress a balance of power tilted in favor of the insiders, a kind of intermittent ground swell rolling in from the rural West against the money power and entrenched positions of the industrial East.

If Populism had a distinguished ancestry, it also had a future. Much of the Populist program was enacted by states and by the nation in the twenty years following the party's formal burial. Among families like the Johnsons the tradition flowed on; the programs might change, but the sentiments behind them did not. In Johnson's case, even the programs he supported were in some cases the same as those of his father's generation. A few weeks after he became a Congressman, in 1937, Johnson voted for an extension of low interest rates on federal farm loans against the wishes both of President Franklin D. Roosevelt and of Johnson's key supporter, House Majority Leader Sam Rayburn of Texas. The purpose of young Johnson's first visit to the White House was to persuade President Roosevelt to authorize federal loans for getting dams built and electricity carried into his region of Texas; national aid to irrigation had been one of the planks in the Southern Alliance's Populist platform forty-seven years before. Now, thanks to Johnson's persistence, it wasn't long before flood-control works were being built on the Pedernales River and a sign was erected outside Johnson City reading: "The Most Electrified City in the West." The day electricity came to Blanco County was one of the proudest days in Lyndon Johnson's life. A plaque outside the Pedernales Electric Cooperative reads (with that lack of mealy-mouthedness that the President likes references to his achievements to display): "*A Product of the Faith, Ability and Foresight of Lyndon Baines Johnson While Congressman Tenth District 1938.*" With electricity the income of the region jumped almost overnight, and Johnson acquired locally a patriarchal status that he has never lost. As an elderly Negro in Austin remarked recently, "This place has certainly jumped ahead mightily since Lyndon went to Washington."

It is thus not surprising that if Johnson believes in anything he believes in the efficacy of government. His incredible campaign tours, when he calls on the folks to "come and hear the speakin,'" rambles on about making America a better land and about his ambition to be the "President of all the people," and then plunges into the crowd to emerge elated, with his hands and wrists aching from handshakes—all this seems to be connected with a desire to reproduce on a national scale what he has achieved in his dirt-poor region of Texas.

It is evident that this desire owes much to the Populist strain in Johnson. It also seems likely that the paradoxes of Johnson's unusual character are to be looked for in the same area. If he has in the past seemed too conservative for the taste of Northern Democrats, and yet has subsequently surprised them by his liberalism, it is surely in part because his liberal attitudes grow from some very antique American roots. If he feels an outsider in Washington although it has been his stage for thirty-five years, it may be because he still cannot believe that all those East-Coast sophisticates understand in their bones, as he feels *he* understands, what the real America is like—was not Kennedy a Senator before he even visited the prairie states? If he still feels suspicious of Eastern bankers and yet makes them members of his task forces, may this not be because his head tells him that times have changed, even in banking, but that his guts tell him that his father's friends were right? If he distrusts Eastern intellectuals and yet had Bundy at his right hand, may it not be because he is still heir to the Populist conviction that the judgment of the common man is as sound as that of the learned, though at the same time his experience has taught him to respect trained intellectual caliber?

Between the thin, eager, young Populist and hundred-per-cent New Dealer in Washington during the thirties and the wily President of today, there lies the war and the period when Johnson established his mastery of Congress. It is typical of Johnson's "middle period" that both his war career and his Senate career have faint question marks hanging over them.

In 1942 he was sent by President Roosevelt to Australia on a trip to inspect United States forces, and while there flew on a bombing mission to New Guinea. For this he was awarded the Silver Star, the third highest decoration in the United States, by General MacArthur. He wears the medal regularly in his lapel and occasionally has drawn attention to it when criticized for making the decisions on bombings in Vietnam himself instead of leaving them to the military on the spot. Accounts of the trip that preceded the award differ, however. Foster Hailey has written in the *New York Times:* "Mr. Johnson made the mission in a plane piloted by Lieut. Walter Greer of Russelville, Ark., who was later killed in a bomber crash in the States in 1944. Its crew had named the B-26 the 'Heckling Hare.'"

A dispatch of June 10 to the *New York Times* from Byron Darnton, its correspondent who later in 1942 was killed in action off New Guinea, indicated that Mr. Johnson's plane was *not* involved in a battle with a group of Japanese Zero fighters over Salamaua and Lae. A long article appearing in the newspaper on June 12 reported the fight engaged in by the other planes on the mission. Mr. Darnton wrote: "The plane (in which Mr. Johnson was riding) developed mechanical trouble and was forced to return without reaching its target. But the Representative got a good first-hand idea of the troubles and problems confronting our airmen and declared himself impressed by the skill and courage of the bomber crews and fighter pilots." Mr. Darnton's dispatch passed through censorship, and some passages may have been cut or altered. Other accounts say that the plane was attacked by eight Zeros and was hit repeatedly by cannon and machine-gun fire.

Six years later, after five terms in the House, Johnson entered the Senate after a primary, tantamount to election, in which he beat the Texas governor, Coke Stevenson, by an extremely narrow margin. His opponents said it was rigged, but his opponents, naturally, were biased. As V. O. Key, a student of Southern politics, has explained:

The most famous of all Texas machines is that of the Parr family in Duval County. It gained in national prominence in 1948 along with the neighboring Jim Wells County when Lyndon Johnson won the second senatorial primary by a state-wide margin of 87 votes. . . . The boss of Duval and the leader in the 18-county twenty-seventh senatorial district is George Parr, rancher and oil operator, who inherited his domain from his father, Archie, the "Duke of Duval."

Following the 1948 election George Parr took offense at complaints by Stevenson about bloc voting in Duval and surrounding counties. He pointed out that in four previous elections Stevenson had solicited his support and his counties had gone for Stevenson with about the same enthusiasm they showed for Johnson this time. "And I never heard a complaint from him about the bloc vote in Duval County."

Thus the widening of his base in Texas brought

Johnson up against some of the roughest, most eccentric, and most corrupt politics in the United States, and his entry into big-time politics—he was re-elected to the Senate with an overwhelming majority in 1954—seems to have begun a hardening process in Johnson which gave his character the scars it now so plainly carries. Very few people know the full story of his activities in Texas during those years, but it wasn't all visits to the First Christian Church in Johnson City. Somewhere along the way, he lost his illusions; and the ideals he had learned from his mother disappeared from public view.

IN the Senate Johnson became completely an operator, standing for action, for government, for getting legislation through, sacrificing everything to achieving the mastery of the Congressional machine. In the opinion of one of his old cronies, Johnson at some point deliberately decided "that he couldn't be both a legislative leader and a man of principle. In the Congress, the key to successful leadership is usually a matter of getting a small group of people to vote a particular way. Principles make it impossible. You have to choose which kind of politician you're going to be." Johnson made his choice, and, having done so, established a voting record of tactical mobility that still causes him public—and, conceivably, private—embarrassment, particularly on the civil rights issue.

Running the Senate as Democratic Majority Leader under Eisenhower, he became the second most powerful man in the country. "He owed his success to three factors," explains a lawyer who worked with him in his Senate office, "sheer work, his drive to personal achievement, and his immaculate knowledge of the buttons to push. He was very good, too, at using experts; he used to throw them, I remember, by asking them what effect their proposals would have on the daily lives of the people. His moods were variable in those days too: it depended on whether he had anything on his mind."

Another aide remarks: "He was both the son of the Senate and the father of it, responsible for many of its procedures. That was the difference between him and Kennedy. Kennedy was just traveling through on his way to the Presidency, and the Senate resented it; some of his measures were stopped from sheer spite."

Even so, despite Johnson's dominance of the Senate, he thought he could never be President. As Kennedy remarked in 1960, he, Kennedy, was the best qualified Presidential candidate in the country, "except for Lyndon—and he hasn't got a chance." He "hadn't got a chance" because he came from the South, and no Southern candidate in modern times had been elected President. Johnson himself bitterly recognized the fact. He still believes that regional prejudice, in the 1960 election, was more important than religious bigotry—that is, regional prejudice stopped him, but religious bigotry didn't stop Kennedy. Not all Johnson's friends take the same view. When he was making up his mind to go for the Presidential nomination, one or two of them tried to persuade him to make some big liberal speeches, particularly on civil rights, to gain support in the Northern cities. Johnson ruminated and decided against it—partly because he thought that the big speeches might weaken his base in the Senate, and partly because he thought it wiser to hang back and wait for Kennedy and Hubert Humphrey, his two main opponents for the nomination, to knock themselves out. Some of his friends think that if he had taken their advice he would have won. Instead, having lost, he accepted Kennedy's offer of the Vice-Presidency.

According to Professor Schlesinger's published report, Kennedy made this offer only tentatively, and Johnson "grabbed it." Perhaps; but it would be surprising if the offer had not been perfectly genuine. It was, after all, a sensible one to make. Kennedy respected Johnson and reckoned he would help the ticket more in the South than he would damage it in the North. The calculation was correct; without Johnson, Kennedy would have been beaten. What is certainly true is that Johnson was surprised at being offered the job, and Kennedy was surprised at Johnson's acceptance. Even now, Johnson's motives aren't clear, for he must have thought he was giving up a kinglike status as the leader of the Senate for the far less important role of Vice-President. One old friend said not long ago that Johnson's motives were so complicated he wouldn't even begin to describe them, but fatigue played a part, and so did Johnson's desire to be a national, as distinct from a Southern and Senatorial, figure.

There must have been many times when Johnson regretted his decision. Kennedy himself treated Johnson well. Their initial wariness turned to mutual regard, and Kennedy insisted that Johnson be kept informed about everything that was afoot. But Johnson must have been pained by the devotion Kennedy so easily aroused; he must have been profoundly hurt by the way the Kennedy clan, and the Kennedyites in the White House, treated him as a hangover from what they considered the grimy pre-Kennedy days; and he must have been bitter at having to sit and watch, barely consulted though he knew he could do better, while Kennedy ran into legislative difficulties with Congress.

These painful years were chiefly useful to Lyndon Johnson in giving him several trips overseas with Mrs. Johnson at his side, allowing him to glimpse the great twentieth-century division between nations—the gulf between the rich and poor. He has always had a deep compassion for the poor, and his sight of the Middle East in particular moved him greatly—"There was nothing phony about that," remarks one associate. Almost as important, these journeys abroad also helped to prepare Mrs. Johnson, an enthusiastic and observant tourist, for her coming role as First Lady.

Mrs. Johnson has always had an important influence on the President. Seeing her smiling, a shade unnaturally, among a crowd of strangers, and knowing her record of attendances at women's luncheons, her facility for small talk, and her published recipes for Snappy Cheese Rolls and Pedernales River Chili, it would be easy to mistake her for a super-American clubwoman. Or again, on the evidence of the Musak booming out of the trees on the ranch, and the find-your-partner guessing games that she used to favor as an ice-breaking prelude to meals, some Washingtonians have classified her as a provincial who has struck it rich. Indeed, the entertainments at the White House for visiting foreigners have seemingly shown her out of her depth as the successor to Mrs. Kennedy. One Japanese lady, asked her view of a singer, illuminated by revolving colored lights, who had been hired to amuse the Japanese Prime Minister, said she supposed the choice had something to do with the "inscrutable West."

Others, noting Mrs. Johnson's single-minded devotion to the advancement of Lyndon Johnson—shown most strikingly in her vigorous, well-planned, and effective campaign trips—identify her as the drive behind the President. "I think of them," remarked a sharp-tongued wit recently, "as the Macbeths." Mrs. Johnson, however, is not to be fitted into any of these categories; she is almost as many-sided as her husband. The neatest capsule summary of her character was devised by Adlai Stevenson, who called her "beguiling and efficient."

She comes from a gentler and more prosperous background than the President. Her mother died when she was five, so that she was compelled to be self-reliant from an early age. Her father was a storekeeper and landowner in East Texas, owning eighteen thousand acres farmed by tenants; and she had a charge account at Neiman-Marcus in Dallas at a time when Lyndon was still sweeping floors to help pay his way through Texas State Teachers College. Mrs. Johnson has said that she had neither swept a floor nor cooked a meal when she married him in 1934. It was her family who financed the first step in Johnson's political career; her father lent him $10,000 to enable him to fight his 1937 campaign for Congressman.

The President evidently remains deeply dependent on his wife. There are those who say that in a sense she is the second most important person in the White House, not because she drives him, which is unnecessary, but because he turns to her often for advice, knowing that it will be shrewd and impartial. Unlike the President, she is known for her well-controlled temper; White House aides claim that he is calmer if she is around than if she is out of town, when he becomes resentful and restless.

Her energy is prodigious—like Churchill, she "packs her day like a trunk"—and her talents are various. It may or may not be true that undue influence helped her to secure the television franchise that enabled her to expand her small radio station in Austin (bought for $17,500 in the middle of the war) into a large business with more than a hundred employees, an $800,000 headquarters, other satellite television stations in other parts of Texas, and a slice of Austin real estate, the value of the whole estimated, as of 1964, at as much as seven million dollars. Again, it may or may not be true that her husband has given her more of a hand behind the scenes with the company than has ever been visible on the surface. Even so, it was Mrs. Johnson's own money (she is reported to have inherited some $70,000, plus 3,800 acres in Alabama, from her mother's family) that she put into the original radio station, which was in debt when she bought it; and it was her personal, detailed control of the company's expansion that ran up the millions.

Her political acumen is plainly as acute as her financial skill. It was acquired not in drawing rooms but out on the stump in Texas and in legislative committee rooms in Austin, and its practical nature is evident in two captions she has written in one of her many scrapbooks. Under a photograph of the President, showing him speechmaking, she has written, "This may influence some voters"; under a second, showing him shaking hands, she has added: "This surely does." She once told a friend, discussing the hordes of visitors from Texas she was required to show around Washington in the days when Johnson was a Senator: "I particularly enjoy a visitor who wants to go to a Senate hearing," a remark that recalls the political zest shown by Johnson's mother half a century earlier when she was taken as a girl to hear William Jennings Bryan address the Texas Legislature. Besides zest, Mrs. Johnson has considerable political courage. During the 1964 Presidential campaign, when she undertook a whistle-stop tour on the President's behalf in the Southern states, she must have recalled the dangerous moment in the 1960 campaign when she and her husband were mobbed by a hostile crowd yelling,

"Traitor," and "Civil rights," and she herself was hit on the head by an insulting placard.

As First Lady, after an initial pause for stock-taking, Mrs. Johnson rapidly found for herself a genuinely useful role, which may also be politically helpful to her husband, assisting children from poor families under the Poverty Act, and organizing her more famous beautification program. These activities are shrewdly chosen: neither is directly political; both are appropriate to a First Lady; neither invites comparison with the achievements of her predecessor, Mrs. Kennedy; and both are self-evidently worth doing. When she stops her car to alight and pick up a discarded Coke bottle, the cynical are inclined to mock; but the beautification trail ahead of the discarded bottles leads into a jungle where some powerful interests lurk, from billboard owners to real-estate men. It may be assumed, however, that Mrs. Johnson knows precisely what she has taken on.

Whether Mrs. Johnson knew what she was taking on when she married Lyndon Johnson, however, is more doubtful. She admits, publicly, that he is still capable of astonishing her. This is equally true of others close to him; even now, very few of them seem to be certain that they have got his measure or are confident that they understand him, and no one seems ready to predict what effect six and a half more years (the President's reasonable expectation of office) in control of the monstrous apparatus of American power will do to a man with his peculiar psychological make-up. Even so, the people who are still alarmed by him or skeptical of his ability appear to be judging the animal by its behavior in the paddock rather than by its form on the track.

There can no longer be reasonable doubt about Johnson's sheer ability. There has been no real ground for doubt from the beginning. When Kennedy was assassinated, Johnson was faced with the most sudden and rigorous test of an incoming President's nerve and caliber that could have been devised, short of a Cuba-type international crisis. Everyone who watched him from inside the White House, including the Kennedyites, agrees that his performance in those early days was almost flawless. Since then, he has set in motion what has been widely described as a domestic revolution. No one could show his exceptional skill and yet be a stupid and unaware man, or a crude thinker.

Nor can it be taken for granted that he is a President who acts impulsively, as some critics have charged. On domestic matters there is ample evidence to the contrary, that he makes decisions slowly. On foreign affairs, the episodes usually adduced to support the impulsiveness theory do not, in fact, appear to do so. Necessarily, this evidence comes from within the Johnson Administration, and is therefore biased. Even so, it leaves the theory unproved, at the least. What it does indicate is that Johnson may tend to allow domestic political considerations too much force in taking foreign-policy decisions.

First, there is the cancellation of the state visits to Washington of President Ayub Khan of Pakistan and Prime Minister Shastri of India. The usual explanation here is that Johnson simply blew his top at the prospect of being lectured on his own doorstep about Vietnam by two Asians. In the White House one is offered a different perspective. The visits were arranged down the line in the bureaucratic machine and came up desk by desk to the President. The arrangers of the visits had their timetable, which was that of people who are always setting up state visits; but the President had a quite different timetable, which was that of a legislator. Johnson was trying to get a foreign-aid Bill through Congress. He considered that it would be better for him, and incidentally better for Shastri and Ayub Khan, if the visit were delayed until after the Bill, instead of taking place while the Bill was going through: Shastri talking about Vietnam, and Ayub Khan discussing his visits to Peking would not, the President felt, encourage Congress to hand out money. Soundings, accordingly, were taken in Delhi and Karachi; the respective American ambassadors were shocked; the press heard about it; and there was uproar.

Second, there is the Dominican Republic. In this episode the President's decision to land twenty thousand American troops is said to have been motivated by nothing more complicated or more sophisticated than the thought that it was better to move in strength at once, and disentangle later, than to risk finding himself with another Castro—or someone the Republicans could describe as another Castro—in an area of high political sensitivity.

It seems possible that these explanations, which have Johnson paying more attention to domestic than external considerations, are not too far from the truth. For the first, and perhaps the last, point about Johnson is that he is above all a political animal. He does not have an exclusive private vision of the future. He is a man who fixes things up, who knows what will work, who is familiar with the relation between the moving parts of the entire American political machine, and who can calculate how much oil poured into what sump in Washington will make which wheels go round in Wyoming or Arkansas. If he can, he avoids a fight. If he can, he negotiates. And when he negotiates, he settles for what he can get. He seems to resemble his only hero, Franklin Roosevelt, more than he resembles his immediate predecessors. Like Roosevelt, he sometimes works both sides of the street—pursues two alternative policies at the same time with different groups. Like Roosevelt, he has his eye on the next step, rather than any long-term plan. Like Roosevelt, he sometimes takes a subterranean route

74

to his objectives. He can be doing one thing on the table with his hands, and another thing under the table with his feet.

Johnson's selection of Senator Hubert Humphrey as his Vice-President is a case in point. Throughout the summer of 1964, before the Presidential campaign began, the nation waited for him to announce his choice of Vice-President, who might also be his successor. The months dragged on, and Johnson appeared to be veering now toward this candidate and now toward another, until at last, in late August, he announced that he had chosen Humphrey. Yet some people near the President now think it obvious, looking back, that he had made up his mind by the preceding Easter. Between Easter and August he encouraged people of all sorts to come and urge him to choose Humphrey.

This sort of maneuver in search of his beloved "consensus" comes naturally to Johnson. He is, by trade, a conciliator. Everyone in Washington was bored long ago by the word consensus, but it does indicate what the President is after—to an extent, possibly, that still causes him to feel that his real job as President is to improve the conditions of life within the United States, not the world outside.

In his pursuit of national unity at home, for instance, possibly one of his most fruitful achievements has been to persuade American business that he is on its side. Considering that, simultaneously, he has been sponsoring a legislative program of Medicare (formerly known as "socialized medicine"), education, anti-poverty bills, and federal housing subsidies—measures of the very kind that American business has traditionally bewailed as death blows to the free enterprise system—this is a truly remarkable piece of legerdemain. Broadly speaking, American business hated Roosevelt, disliked Truman, and distrusted Kennedy—especially after he called the steel men "sons of bitches." But Johnson, a close associate of all three, has persuaded them that the conservation of human resources that would otherwise be wasted is as important to the health of the free-enterprise American economy as the exploitation of natural resources, and will in the long run show just as tangible results in the Wall Street stock market.

Johnson seems to want to address himself to the

serious domestic problems. None is more serious within the United States than the Negro problem, which lies like a time bomb in the foundations of American society. Can 160 million whites amalgamate with 20 million blacks? Can the effacement of political inequality from American laws be followed by the revolution in manners required to eradicate inequality from American society? Or will the Negro's quickening demand for equality disrupt the nation? The President has shown every sign of wishing to tackle seriously the most difficult domestic task any American Administration has undertaken since Lincoln saved the Union. As a Senator, Johnson did more than any other man to break up the solid South on the Negro question. As President, he has completed legislation designed to assure all Negroes of their full political rights. Now he has committed his Administration to an attack on the tremendous, and possibly hopeless, task of transforming the Negro's place in society, which is intimately related to the scarcely less tractable problems of the American poor and the decaying American cities. Johnson, the Southerner, has made a commitment that would have been inconceivable for Kennedy, the Northerner. He may indeed be said, without exaggeration, to have appointed himself the leader of the Negro cause. He seems determined to tackle nothing less than the corrosive legacy of slavery.

If Johnson has surprised people by his attitudes to business and the Negroes at home, he may conceivably surprise them also, in the long run, over foreign affairs and Communism. He is not a cold warrior. When he came to office, he did his utmost to continue the *détente* with the Soviet Union begun by Kennedy and Khrushchev. He regards any deterioration of American-Russian relations since he has taken office as entirely the fault of the Russians. He thinks that Communism has changed, and he feels it will change further, given time. He would agree profoundly with de Tocqueville that "the democratic revolution is the most permanent tendency to be found in history." He does not share the old ostrich-like American attitude to Communist China. Had it not been for the rising tide of the Vietnam war, he would, in the opinion of some of his advisers, have gone further than Kennedy in favoring the admission of China to the United Nations. He is prepared, if he ever gets the chance, to deal with China as a great power. The United States has a complete, trained staff ready to move into an embassy in Peking.

He would like to trade with the Eastern bloc, and he could see no ideological bar against making, in the spring of 1965, his offer to invest a billion dollars in a cooperative development scheme in Southeast Asia that would include the North Vietnamese. At the same time, he shows "a rather fierce determination," as one of his aides put it, to withstand Communist aggression. He would find it hard to define what he means by "aggression," or to establish criteria by which it may be identified when it occurs; he would certainly say, however, that it has taken place, during his term of office, in the Dominican Republic and in Vietnam.

There seem to be two contrary sides of Johnson's nature at work here, operating within the system of necessity that has trapped him in Vietnam. On the one hand, he would ideally like to do business with anyone. On the other hand, he is like a man on a frontier trail who feels that he must be constantly on the alert in case someone jumps him.

He is a wary man, but his wariness is different from caution. This is where his tendency to create problems where none exist—at least in the form in which he thinks they do, as with the Dominican Republic —gets him into difficulties.

He prides himself on his capacity to absorb verbal insults from foreigners without answering in kind. But when he believes that action is being taken against the United States he becomes like the Texan horned toad which, when attacked, shoots blood out of its eyes. When the Russians fired on an American aircraft in the Berlin corridor, he reacted very strongly. When North Vietnam patrol boats attacked Sixth Fleet destroyers, he struck back at their bases. "Drop your gun, then we'll do business," seems to be one of his basic attitudes. When the Panamanians rioted over what they regarded as an insult to their flag, and the Government of Panama subsequently broke off relations with the United States and demanded renegotiation of the Canal treaty, Johnson, with un-Kennedy-like roughness, said that the United States would discuss nothing until relations were restored, but that then they would discuss anything. In this instance, as with the cancellation of the Shastri visit, the President has appeared to pay little regard to any sensibilities that might be wounded by the execution of what he regarded as the correct American policy.

Even so, in foreign as in domestic affairs, one of his strengths is his politician's capacity to identify with the other person's problems and pressures. He has tried to avoid increasing Russia's difficulties over Vietnam. He has shown understanding about the British Prime Minister's back-benchers. He soon realized that the problem in Vietnam was to disentangle not only without disgrace to the United States but also without disgrace to China. It is entirely possible, however, that as a man who matured in the 1930's he does not fully comprehend the kind of forces that are loose outside the United States in the 1960's. Despite a lifelong acquaintance with Mexicans in his home State of Texas, he may not appreciate the cultural hostility that Latin Americans feel toward Americans. Similarly, it is doubtful whether he understands what fuels the spirit of Asian nationalism. He feels an outsider and an underdog himself—yet does not seem able to realize that others may regard him in another light.

He seems to have been at fault, too, in condoning certain weaknesses within the actual structure of the Administration. For instance, it was commonly said in Washington for a long time after Johnson had settled in that he needed a new Secretary of State. Mr. Rusk, though patient and lucid, was widely regarded as a weak man. President Kennedy used to wish that he would speak out more boldly, and Secretary McNamara was said to wish the same. As it was, the politics of the war in Vietnam got less attention at the President's level than the military needs—a mistake perhaps made first by Kennedy and inherited, without being corrected, by Johnson.

Why then did Johnson not replace Rusk? The answer may lie in Johnson's loyalty to those who are loyal to him. Rusk, when Johnson was Vice-President, treated him well and kept him informed. That alone might not have been enough to save him, if he had not come under fire during the summer of 1965 from those whom Johnson regarded as his enemies. When that happens, Johnson closes ranks. "He believes," said one of his aides, "in solidarity."

The President is not the sub-Goldwaterite he has been taken for. At no stage in the White House has there been hysteria over Vietnam, or any sign of a desire to teach the Communists a lesson once and for all. The President knows now, if he did not know before, that the world is not so simply put to rights. The steady buildup of American forces that continued throughout 1965 was undertaken, evidently, with the greatest reluctance, while the President searched for a compromise as never before. As his third year of office began, there seemed every reason to suppose, always granted that a way out of the Vietnam involvement could be found, that the world would increasingly find Lyndon Johnson a healing influence.